Lionheart

Published by Accent Press Ltd – 2014

ISBN 9781783754892

The Quick Reads project in Wales is an initiative coordinated by the Welsh Books Council and supported by the Welsh Government.

Printed and bound by CPI Group (UK) Ltd, Croydon, CR0 4YY

Cover design by Midnight Designs

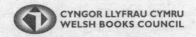

CYNGOR LLYFRAU CYMRU
WELSH BOOKS COUNCIL

Noddir gan
Lywodraeth Cymru
Sponsored by
Welsh Government

Lionheart

Richard Hibbard

With Graham Thomas

ACCENT PRESS LTD

Quick Reads 2014

Congratulations on choosing a 2014 Quick Read.

The Quick Reads project, with bite-sized books, is designed to get readers back into the swing of reading, and reading for pleasure. So we hope you enjoy this book.

What's your opinion?

Your feedback can make this project better. Once you've read one of the Quick Reads series, visit www.readingwales.org.uk or Twitter #quickreads2014 to post your feedback.

- Why did you choose this book?
- What did you like about it?
- What do you think of the Quick Reads series?
- Which Quick Reads would you like to see in the future?

What next?

Once you've finished one Quick Read – have you got time for another?
    Look out for other titles in the 2014 Quick Reads series.

Chapter One

GROWING UP

If it was ever going to happen, it would have happened then.

I had just helped the British and Irish Lions win a Test series in Australia, my tackle had crumpled their key player, and a picture of me celebrating with James Bond actor Daniel Craig, had been beamed around the world. It was my moment in the sun.

But it didn't happen that night, or the next. Just as it didn't happen after I won my first cap for Wales in 2006.

All my life I've been waiting for the phone to ring and for the bloke on the other end to tell me he was my dad. I don't know who he is or where he is. I don't know if he's still alive, or whether he even knows about me. The only certainty is that if the phone rang and he wanted to meet me, I'd agree.

After that, I don't know. A handshake ... maybe an awkward conversation. After which, I've no idea. Maybe I'd thump him for all the

1

grief and struggle he'd caused Sibs. Who knows?

My mother never really talked about my father and I never really asked. Growing up, that's just the way it was. It wasn't discussed. Sometimes I used to imagine the phone at home might ring and he'd be on the other end, with some kind of explanation. But the call never came.

For the first few years of my life, I assumed my dad was the same guy as my brothers' dad. I can't remember exactly how the news was broken to me that, in fact, that wasn't the case. I think it was blurted out by one of my brothers during an argument. I'm told I have half-sisters through my dad, but I don't know anything about them and have never met them.

My wife, Louise, is probably more curious about my father than I am these days. I'm lucky that her dad is like a father to me. But I suppose I have always been seeking a father-figure in my life. I suppose I still am.

Sibs was my mum. Or Siriol Hibbard, to be precise. Me and my three brothers called her Sibs. My brothers' mates called her Sergeant Sibs because she was hard as nails and they were terrified of her.

I'm from Fairfield, one of the rougher areas in the middle of Port Talbot. It's near Aberavon Quins Rugby Club.

I lived opposite the comprehensive school, St Joseph's. I was born in Neath Hospital in 1983 and I went to Sandfields Primary, which is in Fairfield.

I have three older brothers. Nicholas is the oldest, then Matthew, then Daniel. Nicholas is ten years older than me, Matthew (Ginger) is eight years older, and Daniel is six years older.

I was just a baby compared to those three. Nicholas had a different father from Matthew and Daniel. I had a different father again. My mother was married to Matthew and Daniel's dad, but they split up and she met someone else – my father.

But he was obviously a right beauty and didn't stick around after I came along, for whatever reason. So, growing up, it was just us five.

We lived at 25, Newton Avenue. About three years ago, Ginger bought the house back because we lost it at one stage. Mam had got in a mess with money and didn't pay any bills.

My mother died three years ago. But the good thing was that she'd moved back to that house before she died. She loved it there.

She died young at fifty-nine and very suddenly. There was no period of illness. She was diabetic and a big lady, but she rode a bike and seemed pretty healthy. Ginger was living with her, and one night he said she was feeling unwell. They took her into hospital and at 3 a.m. I had a phone call telling me I had better go there.

By the time I got there she had died – which was the worst part of it, the fact that I didn't get to see her.

It was tough because I'd had a brilliant pre-season and was in the best shape I'd been in for years. Her death knocked all that out of me. They were a difficult few months.

For two weeks after she died I would wake up at 3 a.m. every morning – the exact time I'd had the phone call. It wasn't a nice time.

My brothers were all rough, tough boys and my mother had to be pretty tough herself to put up with all of us. And they had their mates, some of whom were even worse.

We had a wall outside our house which got knocked down four times by joyriders, mostly mates of my brothers trying to show off. It was a well-known area for nicking cars.

Our house was a semi-detached, right next

to all the prefab houses – or the 'tin houses' as we called them. You can see the school I lived opposite from the M4. Being so close to the motorway, sometimes we used to hit golf balls over it. The house had three bedrooms, but one of them was a box room. I shared with Ginge.

Ginge kept himself to himself, but could be a bit nutty every now and again. Daniel and Nicholas eventually ended up in the army.

One of my early memories is of Daniel and his mates trying to toughen me up by laying me on the floor and kicking me. They told me it was to make me harder. I remember one day I went punch for punch on the arm with one of Daniel's friends. I had a bruise on my arm the same size as the tattoo I've got there now. It was massive and my mother went nuts.

My mother protected me a lot from my brothers. Don't get me wrong – they didn't batter me or anything but I did get hit. Luckily I was big for my age – and I needed to be, to cope with those three.

Nick was big, Dan was stocky too, but Ginge was the runt of the litter. I got roughed up at an early age by them and that was pretty much how it went for the next few years.

My father's absence was something that

simply wasn't discussed. Much later on, about five years ago, I sat Mam down and asked her a few questions about him but I didn't get many answers.

It was not as if my brothers saw much of their fathers, either, though. There wasn't really a father figure in our family, only my grandad who lived miles away in Haverfordwest.

My mother's mum was from Yorkshire and lived with my grandad in the house we lived in until she died and Grandad met someone from west Wales. So he gave Mam the house and moved down west. Now and again we would go and stay with Grandad.

The name Hibbard was Matthew and Daniel's dad's name. Jones was my mother's name, but I took her married name, even though I don't really have any connection with the Hibbard family, apart from through my brothers.

My mother used to work as a cleaner in one of the nightclubs in town. She used to take me along, which was good. It was called Wall Street, right in the town centre.

She also worked in play schemes for special-needs kids and used to take me along to those as well. We used to go on some good trips, especially in the summer.

Life was a struggle for my mum with four kids. She got into financial trouble a couple of times and we eventually lost the house.

I was about fourteen or fifteen at the time. We had to move, and ended up only two streets away, which was tough. Nick and Daniel had left by then, so there was just me, Ginge and Mam.

She didn't drive. If we ever went anywhere we used to go on bikes. In rain or shine, we'd go on our bikes – always. We were the bike family – that's how people knew us. That was a bit of a ball-ache, to be honest, but the only alternative was to walk everywhere.

We used to live on the corner at a T-junction. When the temperature dropped, and there was water on the road, cars would skid everywhere coming around the corner. Sometimes my brothers would try to make it smoother and more slippy. Fortunately, there were no real accidents – just people skidding and losing control.

I had a couple of mates who lived a few doors down. They got into a fair bit of trouble.

I also had two friends who lived around the corner. One ended up being a custody sergeant, booking people in at the police station. A lot of

7

those he booked in were other mates of mine or kids who lived nearby!

I had another mate who was in foster care at one point and went off the rails. But he's doing well now as a welder. He was a clever boy, but they had to separate us in school because we were as thick as thieves for a while and got into a fair bit of trouble.

Sandfields Primary and Junior school were on the same site with a playground in between them. My brothers were renowned as tough boys, so their reputation followed me. It was a decent school, but the headmaster – Mr Pemberton – hated me, probably because I wasn't the nicest of kids. We had a few run-ins.

I remember he used to carry this big mobile phone around with him and he'd poke you with it – shove it right into your chest. I didn't like that. He was a right beaut, Mr Pemberton.

But I had some good teachers as well. I still keep in touch with Mr Dwyer even now. He was a good bloke – one of the few I got on with.

It was a fairly rough school with a bit of a reputation. But I suppose I must still like the area, because I've moved only five minutes down the road, where I live with Louise and our two daughters, Tiella and Summer. I don't think

I'll ever leave Port Talbot. All my friends are here and I believe you should never forget where you're from.

My main friends are still non-rugby friends. I don't socialise much with rugby people – at least, not top-level rugby people. Most of my best mates still play rugby for Taibach.

I never really liked school. I think I had ADHD – attention deficit hyperactivity disorder – before it became a well-known condition. Nothing interested me or could keep my attention.

So I never worked at my studies. I was more interested in being Jack the Lad. I always wanted to be a rugby player. My ambition didn't change from primary school through to college.

My college teacher once asked me, "Rich, what are you doing here? You've got no interest in studying." I told him he was right. It was just a back-up plan in case I didn't make it as a rugby player.

I can remember playing only one rugby match for my primary school because I think that was all we had – one tournament played on Aberavon's Talbot Athletic Ground. But we won it and I remember it felt really good.

I lived in front of St Joseph's Comprehensive

School, so at least we had playing fields to play on after primary school. But I didn't end up going to that school because I wasn't allowed in. The headmaster stopped me going there because every time he drove past I used to chuck spuds at his car. I did it as a wind-up. It didn't help my cause that my brothers had knocked the head off the school's statue of St Joseph and, every weekend, they'd also put a can of lager in his hand. If I'm honest, we plagued that school.

When we weren't on their fields playing rugby and football, we were on the school roof chucking stones. They also had an old water tower there which we used to climb. So, I went to Glan Afan Comprehensive School instead.

I had a happy childhood but money was very tight. One of my worst memories is sitting in Aberavon Quins Rugby Club after games as a kid and having no money to buy a can of Coke like all the other boys. I had to rely on their parents to buy me one because I had nothing in my pockets.

It was a horrible feeling and it's stayed with me. Earning decent money was one of the real drivers for me to make it as a professional rugby player. I can remember one day at school a professional rugby player came to help at a presentation. I can't remember who he was, or which team he played for. But it struck me that he drove a nice sponsored car, with big letters down the side, and something inside me twigged that I could be like that.

My mother came to only a handful of games because she thought rugby was too rough and she didn't like it when I got hurt.

I enjoyed playing rugby far more than watching it. I had no real favourite team or players who were heroes to me.

I liked Ieuan Evans, because he scored a try for Wales that beat England, but that was about it.

I never watched rugby. In my house, Ginge had control of the TV set and he only wanted to watch Star Trek.

My brothers weren't really into rugby, although Daniel did get a cap for the Boys Club of Wales. They went a different way to me. I can remember them sitting in Dan's room smoking and me thinking: I don't want to end up like that. There were plenty of opportunities, but I never really touched drugs.

I think my mother knew what they were up to in that room. But she probably took the view that it was safer for them to do it in her house than out on the streets.

I never really fancied taking dope, probably because it would have been so easy and no challenge. All I needed to do was walk into that room.

On Saturday nights, we used to sit on a wall outside and local boys would put a show on. By that I mean they'd nick cars and drive them up and down. Back then cars were just so easy to take.

We lived on a T-junction, so the cars would skid around the corner and our own wall got hit regularly. We'd be sitting on the school wall opposite – crowds of us, watching. That's what passed for Saturday night entertainment in those days.

I never had a go at joyriding myself. I think it was the age gap – my brothers stopped me because they knew I was too young.

Most of those involved were about six years older than me. So I was the little kid who was allowed to watch, but that was it. Bigger boys would sit there, smoking and drinking, waiting for the next car to be driven past.

One night, a boy who had nicked a car wound down the window. "Keep hold of this," he said and handed over a doctor's bag. He'd actually nicked the doctor's car. We hid the bag in a garden. It was all a bit wild.

My brother Nick had a habit of getting drunk and then nicking things. Not stuff from shops, but random things like For Sale signs. One day, my mother woke up and there were about fifty For Sale signs in the house. Nick had been in competition with his mates to see who could collect the most.

He took carpets from the town centre and other stuff, and then one day he came back with a goat.

Nick was wild. He and his mates also made amazing bonfires in the park near our house. They would be so big they would melt the guttering on the houses fifty metres away. They would be collecting wood and tyres for months.

I never actually saw my brothers involved in the car stealing. I only remember them watching. You would see the occasional police car, but not many.

I always used to help Mam do the food shopping. We would get it home and it would then be a choice between eating it all straight away or letting my brothers eat it all straight away.

Mam wasn't the best cook in the world, which is maybe why I rarely suffer food poisoning, wherever I am. I developed an iron-clad stomach.

But my mother needed to eat well to keep her strength up. It allowed her to give us a few beatings if we got too much out of line. She was the only person I was ever really scared of. She wasn't called Sergeant Sibs for nothing.

Nicholas went into the army and Daniel followed him, so then there was just me, Mum, and Ginge. I still didn't get my own room, though, because Dan would claim it when he came home from the army.

Ginge was a tyre-fitter and he was the one who paid for us to have Sky. That gave him control of the only TV in the house, so it meant we watched endless episodes of Star Trek.

Chapter Two

STARTING OUT IN RUGBY

I suppose I was about ten years old when I started to play organised rugby games down at Aberavon Quins.

I was a naturally aggressive sort of person and that dragged me through games when I was a boy. I knew I was a tough kid and I knew I was up against kids who weren't as tough.

Although I was looking for a father-figure, I think what I really wanted was someone to tell me I was doing OK. I had a bit of a difficulty with authority which caused me problems.

I was a prop in those days, but my interest in rugby wasn't really full on. It came and went and so did I.

I wasn't dedicated. I certainly didn't take training very seriously. Maybe I was avoiding the discipline and authority that a proper commitment might have meant.

I was about thirteen or fourteen when the Quins junior section team I played for suddenly folded. So I went to play for Aberavon Green

Stars, but that only lasted a year or so before they folded as well.

That took me to Taibach Rugby Club and it was there that I began to take the game seriously for the first time, at about the age of fourteen. It was difficult because it was quite a walk from my house and Mam didn't have a car.

But I was becoming a better player at school and playing for the older year group. That was giving me a bit more leeway at school with some teachers and made life a bit easier.

I had some decent teachers at that stage, like Mrs Protheroe, and they made me realise I could go one of two ways. I could hang out with the kids who spent all day nicking stuff from shops, or stay on a more acceptable course – certainly in the eyes of other boys' parents, who I was eager to be accepted by. I wanted people to like me.

Deep down I know I was a bit of a bully. My brothers had a reputation and being a tough kid myself it was easy to get my own way if I really wanted to.

At Glan Afan, I knew there weren't many other boys I needed to be scared of. I didn't get into too many fights, but I didn't need to. The family had a reputation, especially Daniel.

I did get into one fight – against a kid from another school who also had a reputation. It was almost an organised event, with other kids standing around watching. There were no words exchanged – just a stare and then we went to it, like a couple of ice-hockey players. It took me a while to get on top, but I think I won eventually, before it was broken up by some passers-by.

I played rugby against the same boy soon after and we ended up having another fight on the pitch. That time, he stormed off and told me he was going to get a knife. Fortunately, he didn't.

I can't say I enjoyed fighting. I wasn't scared of getting hurt, but I was scared of losing. It was a matter of pride.

I was aware that the parents of other boys at Taibach were a bit wary of me. They thought I was bad news even though I didn't really have many fights out on the field. It was a feeling I picked up, so I decided to try to keep myself in check and become more dedicated at rugby. I wanted people to accept me. I wanted to prove I wasn't trouble.

Taibach drew its players from a wider base than the Quins or the Green Stars. It was more like a Port Talbot-wide regional side. And we were good at that youth level. We almost won our league in the first year I was there and managed to win it in the second year without losing a game.

By my third year there, college teams had started to call on our players and the numbers dwindled. We weren't so successful that season, but the important thing for me was that youth rugby allowed me to take the sport seriously. It was well organised and training was rigorous.

By that stage I was even training on Christmas Day morning. I'd also run home from the club.

I went through most of the rugby club initiations at Taibach: first pint, first yard of ale, first tour with proper drinking. But drinking was never that important for me.

In fact, when I was seventeen or eighteen I stopped drinking altogether for a time. I still wanted to go out with my mates, though, so I began working as a bouncer at some of the bars in Port Talbot.

I was the tidy one, the nice guy, if you like. There were others who were less sympathetic to difficult customers. At one place I worked there was a puddle on the rough ground out the back.

Some of the bouncers used to piss in it and if anyone caused any trouble they'd be dragged through that puddle before being sent on their way.

A fair bit of drugs were used by some of the guys I worked with. I remember one of them had to stop working because he was hearing voices.

We used to get paid £40 for the night and free Red Bull. I worked at a pub called the St Oswald's, then the Welcome To Town, then the Carlton. I enjoyed it but I made sure I was off the drink for the whole of that time.

At about eighteen, I had a best mate called Matthew Bradley. We were great friends and used to train together and go out together. That's when I began drinking again, because it was very hard in those days to be involved in a rugby club and not drink. It's much easier now for young players who are in academy environments, but in those days all rugby clubs either revolved around drinking or had a strong drinking culture. That was the way it was. So, although I had decided to try to take rugby seriously, when I stopped working as a doorman I went back to drinking.

My academic career at this stage wasn't

much to write home about. I wasn't interested in school and couldn't find much to motivate me. I left school with a few GCSEs and then a GNVQ in business studies, but not much idea of what I wanted to do. In my last year at school I often wouldn't turn up until 11 a.m. but the teachers seemed to let me get away with it.

I had some ambition to be a fireman, so I went to Neath Port Talbot College, Afan Campus, to study public services. My other option was to follow my brothers into the army. But I didn't have my heart set on exams and things like that.

Aberavon were one of the main rugby clubs in Wales at the time, but I wasn't really interested in watching them. In fact, I had little interest in watching any rugby. I liked playing, and that was it.

For Taibach, we would train on Tuesday and Thursday nights. I was still carrying a bit of extra weight in those days, but nobody seemed to care. I also started playing for Baglan at youth level, which enabled me to play on Sundays as well as Saturdays. One day, though, Taibach played Baglan and I played for Taibach. The Baglan boys obviously didn't think much of that so they battered me. Their props, who were hard boys, took turns in holding me while the other punched me in the head. I was given a proper leathering.

I was capped by Wales Youth at Under-18 level as a prop and that's when it kicked in that I was doing OK at rugby. But although I was training hard there was still something missing from my development as a player. Then one day in youth rugby we met a guy called Phil White. He introduced us to weight training.

After my first weight session, I walked out of the gym and was immediately sick. I could hardly walk. There hadn't been any heavy lifting. It was more of a weights circuit, but my body wasn't used to it and I found it hard.

I got better, though. But I noticed other boys started to drop by the wayside. Eventually, although the whole Taibach Youth team had started with him, it came down to just me and Phil. I became hooked and I'd be phoning him up asking when the next session was. I'd plague him.

I was definitely feeling the benefits of the weights and I was also getting my overall fitness up by running to the gym and then back to the house.

Eventually, I ended up working for Phil in

his window company, so he was a good influence in more ways then one.

After getting my cap at eighteen, I stepped up the weights even more and began to lose a lot of weight. I even moved from prop to the back row.

I knew I was improving, but some things weren't quite what I expected, or even enjoyed.

That Wales Youth cap – which I gained out in Italy in 2003 – proved to be my one and only. I had gone out there carrying a shoulder injury, mainly due to my own stupidity. I had played too many games in the build-up for no other reason than I couldn't say no to teams when they asked.

I liked Taibach and Baglan but Wales Youth was unfamiliar territory for me. It was all different – new team-mates, new coaches, new ways of doing things. I didn't like change. I liked things I knew, things that had become familiar.

It was also a big deal for me just going to Italy. I hadn't travelled much before that and I couldn't afford to take any spending money.

Some of the bigger clubs were now taking notice of me, but I had no means of travelling to see them. I could hardly go those distances on my bike!

Bridgend were keen on me and I went to a few of their training sessions, thanks to the father of a friend who took me in his car. I suppose I should have explained to these clubs that we didn't have a car in our family, but I never did. It wasn't that I was too shy or embarrassed to explain. I just didn't like talking to people. I was anti-social – still am, in many ways.

In my second year of youth rugby, Swansea asked me to go and play for their Under-21 Academy side.

I played a few matches for them, but the club was having terrible financial problems at that time. It was a strange period, because I went straight from youth rugby to playing one match in 2003 for the senior Swansea side against Pontypridd at Sardis Road.

Matthew, my mate, ended up playing three games for the senior team, but I hesitated because I'd started doing something completely out of character for me, something I'm amazed about now when I think back. I'd started watching a little bit of rugby league on TV, and thought it looked exciting. I also felt it suited my style of rugby. So, without any prompting, I decided to email all the rugby league clubs in the north and ask them for a trial.

I had loads of replies. A few said they were interested and one of those was St Helens, who had a contact in Aberavon that they sounded out.

They asked me up for a trial and I stayed there for three weeks. I played in games against Wakefield, Salford and Leeds for the Saints Academy team.

Looking back, I think I turned to rugby league as a result of the Wales Youth appearance not going as well as I had hoped. I felt I'd missed an opportunity, so I looked around for another option.

But I enjoyed my little spell in the north. I stayed in a house with Ade Gardner, the wing who went on to have a great career with Saints and played for Great Britain.

The training was different from rugby union training and I enjoyed it. I didn't know all the rules, but I got by and felt I did OK. St Helens also thought I did OK, but they didn't rush to push a contract under my nose, so I expect they had other possible signings. It also didn't help their interest in me that soon after I came back home I tore ligaments in my ankle.

But I came back with a liking for rugby league, and decided to play for a team that had been created back home, called Aberavon Fighting Irish.

It was a summer league, so I could play rugby union in the winter and switch to rugby league when the union season ended in May.

It was a great crack. Our coach was Chris O'Callaghan, who was a real character. He had coached rugby union at Aberavon. It meant we had a lot of the Aberavon boys playing for the Fighting Irish in the summer.

They took their name from the Aberavon Green Stars and the Irish links with that club. They were crazy – but great fun.

I played that first summer in 2003 and then carried on for a few years after, even though I wasn't officially allowed to. I had to be a bit secretive about my days with the Fighting Irish, so I played under the registered name of Hubert Richards. It was the team manager who dreamed that up. What a genius. Richard Hibbard disguised as Hubert Richards.

I got away with it by the skin of my teeth. I signed for the Ospreys later on and if they had found out I would have been in some serious trouble.

In rugby league I used to play loose forward and loved it. Everything that I really enjoy about rugby union – carrying the ball and smashing into people – you get to do over and over again in rugby league.

I sometimes wonder what might have happened if I'd been offered a deal by St Helens. Maybe I wouldn't have grasped it – because Keiron Cunningham was there at the time – but it's something I've day-dreamed about, playing with Sean Long and all the rest of their great players.

Whether it was risky or not – and whether Swansea and the Ospreys turned a blind eye to it or not – my rugby league summers were definitely helpful. They got me really fit each summer and hardened me up.

By the summer of 2003, I had begun pre-season training with Swansea but there was a great deal of change within the game at that time and regional rugby had arrived.

The Ospreys had been formed from a merger between Swansea and Neath, although both clubs carried on operating club sides under their traditional names in the new Welsh Premiership, below the new regional level.

I played thirty-one matches for Swansea in that 2003–04 season and it was during that time that I was converted from a prop who could also play back row, into a hooker.

Basically the game was changing, and taller players were dominating the back row positions. I was told I could either become an average back row forward or a good hooker. It was an easy choice when they put it like that.

My coaches during that time with Swansea were Keith Colclough and Tony Clement – both great guys and very good coaches.

It was a turbulent time at the club after the creation of the Ospreys. People were still feeling their way. But it was nothing compared to the turbulence created by my attempts to turn myself into a hooker!

It meant learning to throw the ball into the line-out and I was shocking, truly terrible. It was a tough learning period and it would take me four years, and about fifty different throwing techniques, before I really got it right.

I had practised a lot before my first game as hooker, but that didn't stop the whole thing being a nightmare.

Chris Wells, the Ospreys hooker at the time, helped me out. I needed a lot of help. When I threw into the line-out, the ball could literally go anywhere.

In one early game as hooker, I was so bad that my throw didn't even reach the line-out because it struck the back of a prop's head. The touch judge must have felt sorry for me because he let me pick it up and throw it in again!

The idea that I could ever do this for my country, at international level, seemed a million miles away.

Chapter Three

MOVING TO HOOKER

Money was always tight when I was a kid. The food bill was large every week and anything left over just seemed to slip through Mam's fingers.

So, when I was asked to go on a tour to South Africa at eighteen with the old invitational side, Crawshays, it was a bitter-sweet offer. On the one hand, I was desperate to go and play rugby in South Africa, to see if performing overseas might be a better experience than the one I'd had with Wales Youth. But on the other I knew I had no chance of finding the £500 I needed to raise in order to go.

Taibach gave me a few quid but in the end the full £500 was given to me by a random businessman. He was an Aberavon supporter, but I wasn't given his name at the time. He wanted to remain anonymous. But it was a hell of a gesture and it was only a few years later that I actually met him and was able to thank him for his kindness.

I felt nervous about that trip, but it went well and it felt like another hurdle that had been overcome.

I spent a lot of time between the ages of sixteen and twenty playing different types of rugby for various teams and generally doing OK. More important to me than all the various skills I learned was the self-awareness that I was actually decent at this sport – that I could make a crack at it in terms of a career.

I find it difficult to recall individual matches from that period that stick in my mind as significant. I'm not one of those players who remembers every game they have played in, where it was, the scoreline, who scored the tries and kicked the goals. I'm more the guy who forgets the details. For me, past matches seem to merge into one. My memories are sketchy.

I had moved from prop to back row by the time I played a few matches for Taibach Seconds, and then went on to Swansea. It's a big switch from youth to senior rugby, but I found there were older blokes in those senior teams who looked after the younger pups like me. In fact, I felt as though there was some kind of protection order that had been taken out on me. I was kept out of harm's way by blokes who were tough old warriors, guys you wouldn't want to mess with.

When I played prop, I used to enjoy the individual combat of scrummaging. I liked the challenge of trying to out-do the guy you were up against. It would be a personal battle and I liked those. I was never one of those props who got chopsy – I was always too tired – but I did like to stare and smile.

Moving to hooker, the toughest difference in scrummaging is learning how to handle the collapses. Both your arms are trapped so, unlike at prop in a collapse, you are normally falling flat on your face. You can feel incredibly vulnerable. Basically, when you're going down to the ground as a hooker, you tense your neck and hope for the best. It's scary and takes some getting used to. You try not to think about the awful injuries you could possibly suffer to your neck and back, though they are always there at the back of your mind.

For me, the difficulty I was finding in throwing the ball into the line-out took up so much time and energy that I stopped thinking so much about scrummaging terrors. My sweaty nightmares were more about throwing the ball everywhere except where it was meant to go!

I would practise for hours, trying to hit a post. I would spend thirty minutes to an hour in my early days at the Ospreys, starting at seven in the morning. Gruff Rees, who was skills coach back then, would be with me and it would be a case of simply trying to nail it.

Once it clicks, then it clicks, but I found it hard. When Lyn Jones was the Ospreys coach, he wanted shaped, arcing throws. But I couldn't even throw the ball straight down the middle, never mind shape it into an arc. It killed me.

When my throwing-in was poor in a game, it felt like I was walking on quicksand. I would feel myself getting dragged down and there didn't seem to be anything I could do about it. I would pray that we would go for points early on, rather than kick for touch because that would mean me having to find my line-out jumper.

I was so worried about my throwing that I would really try to bust a gut in the rest of my game to make up for it. So, ironically, I would end up getting man-of-the-match awards even though I hadn't been able to throw at all.

The thing about throwing as a hooker is that so much of it is about feel. You are normally aiming at a point that isn't there – throwing at nothing, if you like – in the hope that by the time the ball gets to where it's supposed to be, someone has been lifted up to catch it.

So, it's an act of faith, really … blind faith. It's like falling backwards into someone's arms. You don't know exactly where you're going but you are relying on someone meeting you. They call it "shape throwing" and Lyn was really big on it.

My second rows were generally understanding. They wouldn't moan too much. But the occasions that would really break me was when I'd miss the attacking throws that we really needed.

My throwing wasn't too good in my first couple of seasons at Swansea, but it didn't stop me loving that time of my career. We had a good young side, with some great boys and a very good spirit in the dressing room.

I was so wrapped up in my first season there that I hadn't paid much attention to the wider season of regional rugby. I'm not a big watcher of games and I don't think I had seen a single Ospreys match.

I didn't even know who their players were, apart from the Welsh internationals. But after my first season with Swansea, I was asked to go and see Lyn Jones. My contract with Swansea had been worth around £5,000 a year and it was the first money I'd ever really had from rugby, so it felt like a bonus. I'd done a few odd jobs up until then, alongside my rugby. I was a grass cutter for the council which was good fun except when you worked with a strimmer and you hit the dog mess hidden in the long grass. It would splatter across your visor. And I worked in youth clubs and eventually worked as a teaching assistant – or maybe a bodyguard – at a place where kids were sent after they had been suspended from school.

I had no real qualifications for the job, other than my background in youth clubs which dated back to the time I used to go to them as a kid. I once won Young Achiever of the Year award through working in youth clubs, although I was never really sure why I'd deserved it. But I did spend a lot of time in youth clubs as a teenager and that led into other roles.

Working as a teaching assistant was really enjoyable and in the early days I managed to make everything fit around my rugby. I'd be working normal school hours and then trained in the evenings. I was young and it was easy enough.

But when the Ospreys offered me a contract I had to make a choice. This was a chance to be a full-time professional rugby player, but meant giving up the school assistant work. In truth, it didn't take me long to decide. Being a professional rugby player had been my goal for years.

My meeting with Lyn was short and to the point. He told me I could be a decent hooker and outlined his plans for me as an Ospreys player. He showed me the figures on the contract, but to be honest I didn't really care what they were. I would have signed for nothing. It wasn't a huge step up from the money I was on at Swansea, but it was the first step on the ladder and it was just great to have made it.

Things had been going well with Swansea and I was able to carry on playing for them for most of that season. Generally, I would sit on the bench for the Ospreys on Friday nights – while Barry Williams carried on as hooker – and then be available again for Swansea on the Saturday afternoon.

Barry was ten years older than me and massively experienced. He had been an international player for six years prior to regional rugby and toured with the Lions to South Africa in 1997. He was good to me when I first arrived at the Ospreys – helpful and generous with his advice to this new kid who knew nothing.

Over time our relationship changed, as he saw me as more of a rival. But that's always the way inside a rugby squad, when you're trying to keep someone from taking your place.

Barry knew I wasn't the best of throwers in those days. When I was throwing in training he would come over and say things to put me off. He was crafty, Barry. He used to call himself the Daddy and he was a hugely influential figure at the Ospreys.

There was also Huw Bennett, the other hooker, who was also ahead of me in the pecking order and someone I'd have to battle with over the next few seasons.

I found the full-time training at the Ospreys pretty hard at first. It was a new level of fitness for me, on top of trying to memorise whole patterns of play, and where I was supposed to be after four phases of play. I wasn't used to all that.

Then, there were the analysis sessions to get used to. I remember in the early days arriving very early for one of those and sitting down. The other players arrived in ones and twos and soon it became obvious there weren't enough chairs. Seeing Barry standing, Lyn looked at me and said, "Get up and let one of the real players sit down." That really cut me, which I suppose was the point of it.

Lyn was great at those kind of wind-ups. You could never tell whether it was meant seriously or in jest. I think the aim was to make you try to guess which, and this is unsettling for a new player low on confidence.

Things ticked along until the December of that 2004–05 season when both Barry and Huw got injured. I was told I was starting against Munster, away. I had just turned twenty-one and suddenly felt more nervous about playing a rugby match than I'd ever felt before.

The game was down at Musgrave Park in Cork and it was a notable match as Ryan Jones, who had just broken into the Wales team, was sent off for stamping. Before the game I was worrying, as ever, about my throwing. At that stage I was still a long way from mastering it. It was like a dodgy golf swing. Sometimes it would be fine, but on other days it would be all over the place and I never knew exactly why.

So I was concerned the old sinking sand would take me under. Even these days I can still get worried about that. I think every hooker will admit to it if he's honest.

You can miss one bad throw and shake it off. Even two bad throws in succession is bearable. But if you throw three poor ones it feels like you're going under the waves. You tense up and your hands feel as if they don't belong to you.

But that debut game didn't go too badly. I missed a few line-outs, but not as many as I expected to. I did enough around the park and lasted sixty minutes before they took me off.

I actually enjoyed it. It was the first time I had been involved with a fully prepared, professional rugby operation – with typed notes given to me beforehand about the opposition and my own role – and I enjoyed the level of detail.

We fought hard and only lost narrowly, 13–9, which wasn't bad given that Ryan was sent off. After the game, we went to a bar and I chatted to my opposite number that night, Frankie Sheahan – an experienced Ireland international – which was great. I felt as though I'd arrived somewhere, a place I'd been trying to get to. Happy days.

The next week I was back on the bench. In fact, that was the only start I made for the Ospreys for the rest of that season. Barry was a durable so-and-so and very rarely got injured. I hated him for that.

But I managed to sit on the bench quite a lot for the Friday night games and that enabled me to still play for Swansea on the Saturday in the Welsh Premiership. That meant getting paid by both, which was brilliant. I'd never had so much money, even though it was very modest by other players' standards.

I bought myself a flat in Sandfields. It felt good having my own place and I actually managed to make a few quid by selling it a year later to buy a house. Maybe I'd learnt something from the car experiences.

On the field, things continued to go well for me with the Ospreys. I carried on making the squad as replacement hooker, and gradually began to get more appearances from off the bench.

My only worry was that I was gaining a reputation as an impact player – someone who came off the bench to change things, when I was desperate to become a starting hooker. It would prove to be a tag I found difficult to shake off.

In that first 2004–05 season with the Ospreys, I ended up playing ten games but only one of them was a starting spot – that debut out in Munster. It was frustrating and it carried on into the next season, even though Huw was suffering a lot of injury problems which meant the choice was normally down to me or Barry.

Sometimes, I'd get only ten minutes right at the end. They would call a line-out move, which I'd fail to hit with my throw, and then I'd be back on the bench for the following week and the same thing would happen again. It became a bit of a nightmare, especially when I began to see younger guys coming in to different positions and making the starting line-up.

But Barry was old school. He didn't agree with being rested for any games and never wanted to come off. He was also quick to remind me my throwing still needed plenty of attention.

I had a Player of the Year award from Swansea and I loved the fact I was still able to play for them as well as the Ospreys. They were not as worried about my wayward throwing and that, in turn, gave me more confidence to go out and play well around the field.

I had been a full-time professional rugby

player for a year and felt I had made some big strides. I was much fitter and stronger, thanks to the extra training. I was loving my rugby with Swansea, but desperate to play more often for the Ospreys.

There seemed to be battles to be fought and overcome wherever I turned: getting some starts ahead of Barry and Huw; convincing Lyn I could be trusted to play eighty minutes; avoiding the stick dished out by senior players at training for my dodgy purchases.

But the biggest fights – those that took place inside my own head – were yet to be confronted.

Chapter Four

GETTING THE CALL FROM WALES

Halfway through that second season with the Ospreys, life seemed good. I had a house, a tidy car, and a few quid in my pocket. OK, I wasn't getting the starting appearances for the Ospreys that I was after, but I was playing well for Swansea and getting enough pats on the back from the people around that squad. I was still only twenty-one and felt I was on the right path.

Then, one day, I had a message to attend a meeting with the Ospreys management. Great, I thought, they're going to offer me a new, improved contract.

When I walked into the room, there was Lyn Jones, his assistant Sean Holley, fitness coach Huw Bevan, and the team manager Derwyn Jones. I sat down and waited for the new contract to be put on the table. Instead, they took turns in tearing into me, basically telling me I was rubbish and my attitude was poor. They said if I didn't improve they would release me at the end of the season.

I was stunned – gobsmacked. I thought it was going to be a pat on the head, but it turned out to be a serious ultimatum. I hadn't seen it coming.

I got on to my agent, Rhydian Thomas, and within two weeks a meeting had been arranged with Sale. I met their coaches, Philippe Saint-André and Kingsley Jones, and watched a match up there during a period when Sale had a few Welsh players in their squad.

Sale offered me a contract which was a good one. I didn't actually want to leave but that offer gave me something to bargain with. I told the Ospreys, not entirely certain how they would react, and they insisted they wanted to keep me. As it turned out, the region had a bit of a purge at the end of the season and a lot of boys left, but, thankfully, I wasn't one of them.

It was a time of change. The Neath-Swansea part of the Ospreys' name was dropped but the team's form on the field was excellent and we won the 2005 Celtic League title. I was on the bench as we clinched the championship with a win over Edinburgh at the Gnoll.

I was getting increasingly disheartened, though, because in the following season, 2005–06, although I played eleven matches, I started in only two of them. I was playing against big name, established hookers but just not often enough. It was a hard time.

I wasn't what you'd describe as a student of the game in those days. I wouldn't take much notice of the hookers I was up against. I'd rock up and think about them only when they ran out onto the pitch. It wasn't arrogance – far from it. I think I needed to feel a little unsettled, a bit nervous, to reach my best. "Playing scared" I used to call it. I've spoken to Warren Gatland about it – the little bit extra you find from fear.

But at the end of the 2005–06 season, a strange and unexpected thing happened. I got picked by the Wales coach Gareth Jenkins to go on tour to Argentina. Gareth had seen me come off the bench for the Ospreys and make an impact in games, and he wanted me to do the same for him in South America.

I was twenty-two and felt I had been progressing OK at the Ospreys, even though my opportunities to start games had been limited. I had no real idea of what international rugby was like – certainly no idea of how intense the battlefield can be when you are representing your country.

But then, I had no clue about some of the

other battles I would have to fight over the next few years – the kind of challenges the man in the street doesn't hear so much about. I'm talking about personal battles that go on within your own mind and keep you awake at night.

In my case, my biggest fights have been with injuries, and the demoralising effect they can have on you. And the battle I have often fought with my own weight. For me, those two enemies have sometimes ganged up together to have a real go. That was certainly the case in 2006.

I had been having shoulder problems throughout that 2005–06 season. It was just general wear and tear, but it was getting worse and it very nearly stopped me playing.

The injuries started off with just a general grinding sensation, but that got worse as the season went on. I remember that if my shoulder was just bumped, even by someone off the field, and my arm was in a certain position, the pain in my right shoulder would kill me.

I could live with it, though, and just got through to the end of the season before that Wales tour. I was shocked by my selection for the squad and maybe I felt it was almost unreal. I say that because in the time before we were due to go I stupidly decided to play a game for Taibach Second XV against a touring team from Texas.

I didn't think it would do any harm but I ended up tearing my bicep muscle. A guy's elbow hit me as I tried to go easy on him in a tackle and, 'ping', it was gone.

I thought I'd blown my Wales tour chances because the surgeon, Geoff Graham, told me it would need an operation and then eight weeks' recovery time. I was gutted, totally down.

Geoff did the surgery, but told me afterwards there was good news and bad. The bad was that they had been unable to repair the bicep. The good news was that once the cut healed I could go on the tour.

So, with one good bicep, and the other halfway up my arm, I went on the trip. The bicep is still the same, now. It can't be repaired as the tendon snapped and the ends are frayed like old rope. I've managed to get by as a rugby player, but I do get cramp when I carry shopping bags. At least, that's my excuse. I'm not great at pull-ups, either.

So, I toured. I went to Argentina and won my first Wales cap as a replacement for Matthew Rees on 11 June 2006, in Puerto Madryn. It finished Argentina 27 Wales 25, but I didn't care much about the result if I'm honest. I didn't expect to play. Yet there I was, capped by Wales. Me … Richard Hibbard … a Welsh international.

And it wasn't just me who had a day to remember. James Hook, Alun Wyn Jones, Ian Evans and Rhys Thomas were all capped for the first time that day. We were a long way from home, though, so it felt a little strange. Having said that, it would be a feeling I would have to get used to. It would be another six matches, and three different countries, before I'd get to wear the red jersey in Cardiff.

I'm not an emotional guy. The debut didn't get to me like it does to some players. I was never going to shed a tear over playing for Wales for the first time.

Don't get me wrong. I was desperate to play and even though I suffered food poisoning the night before, they would have had to chop my arm off to stop me playing.

But I didn't feel emotional in the way I get emotional thinking about my family. It's a massive honour, and I'm hugely proud. But nothing to cry about.

I rang home and spoke to my mam that night. She was pleased, but she didn't cry either.

Sibs was like me – rarely emotional about things like that. I think she spent more time telling me her own news.

I really enjoyed both Tests – I came on again in the second in Buenos Aires – and owe a big debt of gratitude to Gareth Jenkins. He didn't last long in the job, but that was only because he was the wrong bloke in the wrong place at the wrong time. He's a very good coach, so passionate about rugby, and I really liked him.

When I came home from the tour, I knew my shoulder was getting worse. It finally went in a tackle against Borders in September and I was told I needed a complete reconstruction. I wouldn't play again until 4 April 2007, some seven months later, and it was the hardest time of my life.

It was my first serious injury and I didn't know how to handle it. I went into steep decline.

They cleaned out the shoulder and tightened the ligaments. Again, it was Geoff Graham who did the op and I got very friendly with him – a great bloke as well as a very good surgeon.

But after the operation, I had no idea about how to handle myself as a long-term injured professional sportsman. I went about it totally the wrong way. Told that I couldn't do anything for six weeks, I started drinking – big time. I was drinking three or four nights a week and I mean hard drinking.

I got back in with all my old mates who enjoyed a drink – guys I hadn't been able to go out with for a while. We drank everywhere – out in Swansea, at home in my flat, anywhere. I wasn't well-known, so it's not as if people were spotting me and asking me why I was out on the beer.

I went from 110 kg to 123 kg in no time at all. The Ospreys noticed … and they went nuts. Lyn would send me emails telling me how overweight I was. He'd then mention that I'd dropped two kilos but put three back on. I must have been a nightmare.

Looking back, this was the start of a serious battle with my weight. I still have to constantly watch what I eat and drink. My wife, Louise, reckons I sleep-eat instead of sleepwalk. I can eat the same amount as her and yet still put on weight.

It's a big problem but is rarely discussed in rugby. I have to be so careful. It's not just the type of food I have to watch, but the amounts.

The Ospreys and Wales weigh me every day, which means there is no escape. I occasionally give up meat for a while – and did so last season – but I've also tried lots of different diets, the quick fixes, which are a total waste of time. They just make your weight yo-yo.

My maximum weight as a player has been 124.5 kg. It was far too big, but I did actually manage to play for Wales at that weight. I hit harder, but I hit far, far, less often. Stamina becomes a big issue at that size.

My top fighting weight is probably 112 kg. I struggle to keep it there – constantly – but I know I'm not alone. Adam Jones is the same. But maybe Adam can get rid of weight more easily than I can. I take the advice of a nutritionist who once told me, "Your diet is a path in the woods. Take one step off the path and you can still see it. But the more steps away you take, the harder it is to see the path."

If things are going well – like after we celebrated the Lions tour – I might have the odd blow-out. I might get through a few pizzas, but I try to stay off the beer.

But back in 2006, all this self-denial was a long way off. I was reckless. I was so heavy when I finally got back to training after that shoulder operation that my back seized up. I could hardly walk to the physio room.

It's easy to drop four or five kilos. That's simple. But the next seven or eight after that are hard to shift. I'm not talking about a short-term battle here. I reckon it took me four years to finally get rid of the weight I put on in that winter of inactivity.

My other problem is my body shape. For some reason, I only seem to carry the weight around my stomach!

Recently, I think I've finally found what works for me – to stick close to that path, not get diverted by temptation, and be constantly aware of any potential pitfalls ahead.

Injuries and weight worries ... weight worries and injuries. That's pretty much what my rugby career has been about. When I've got injured I've put on weight – but when I've lost weight I've sometimes felt vulnerable to injury. It's a vicious circle. I've undergone three shoulder operations and I don't like to think too much about the state they're in.

I didn't cry when I made my debut for Wales, but I'll admit I cried the night I damaged my ankle on the eve of the 2011 World Cup. I had played in that season's Six Nations and when Matthew Rees was ruled out of the tournament it seemed as though I might be the starting hooker.

I had rushed back from another shoulder injury – which in itself had put a big question mark against me going to the tournament in New Zealand – and felt I had turned a corner in terms of my luck with injuries. But in the warm-up match against Argentina that August at the Millennium Stadium, the turf gave way and so did my ankle.

It's still all so clear in my memory – fifty-five minutes on the clock, I stepped back as an Argentine player came into me and went over on my ankle. It seemed innocuous but it was horrendous.

They took me straight for a scan. I went in the car with Carcass (Mark Davies, the Wales physio), and travelling down there I knew things were bleak. There was an awful silence as we drove. It was my first big chance to be the starting hooker at a major tournament and it was going down the drain.

The scans were done at a hospital in Cardiff Bay. There was a bit of milling about, some whispered conversations, and then I asked Carcass, "What are my chances?" He was straight. "No chance," he said. It was a sombre atmosphere and I felt very upset. My ankle ligaments were badly torn and there would be no World Cup experience for me.

What made it worse was that it was meant to have been the shoulder injury that ruined my World Cup, and I had beaten that. I had come back weeks earlier than I was supposed to. People had written me off. So for this new injury to happen just felt brutal. It was a sickener.

It's a lonely place being injured, especially in a team sport. I was on that plane. I was in that squad. It was going to be my first World Cup and then it was shattered. Rugby squads are like families and players don't like to be outside the family. But that's where injury puts you – on the outside. It can get very dark, emotionally.

Louise had been at the game watching and had ended up having to drive my car home. She gave me a big hug when I got back but she felt as awful as me. For a time, she even stopped coming to watch me as she felt she was bringing me bad luck. I'm glad that feeling has gone and she was there in 2013 when we beat England to win the Six Nations, plus she came out for the third Lions Test later that year in Sydney. To have her there felt very special.

So instead of me, Buster (Huw Bennett) went to the World Cup as the main hooker, and had a brilliant tournament. I was really pleased for him because he is a great guy and that tournament was a personal high for him.

Wales took the World Cup by storm and were very unlucky to lose narrowly in the semi-final to France after Sam Warburton was harshly sent off. The excitement of it all came through the TV screen. I would have loved to have been part of it. All over the country, people were going crazy.

But I stayed behind, watched the games on TV alone in the house, and wrote a column for the South Wales Evening Post. It wasn't quite the same.

Chapter Five

PHYSICAL STRUGGLES

After seven months of not playing, not training, and not looking after myself properly following the shoulder operation, I somehow managed to finish the 2006–7 season by getting selected by Wales again to tour Australia.

I had played only a handful of games since returning in the April and I was overweight and under-prepared, but I must have done enough somewhere along the line for the Wales management to think I was worth a punt.

We played the Wallabies in the first Test in Sydney in May 2007 and I was on the bench, with Smiler (Matthew Rees) starting at hooker. We lost 29–23, having been in the lead with only a few seconds left, but I was very pleased to have got on and won another cap.

Matthew then went home as his wife was about to give birth. I had high hopes of starting the second Test, but instead of promoting me they sent home for Mefin Davies.

It felt like a big blow at the time, and I was

gutted. But looking back now, and recalling how huge and overweight I was, it was entirely understandable. I would have done the same thing.

I was young, enthusiastic and would have run through brick walls to play for Wales. But I wasn't dedicated. I just wasn't in shape to play rugby at international level. The speed of the game left me blowing.

But on the strength of that tour, I managed to make the extended 2007 World Cup preparation squad. I still held a dream that I might go to the tournament in France.

When it came to it though, the training camp became something to be endured rather than enjoyed. Early on, I saw a sheet of names for a practice game that seemed to be a list of World Cup probables against possibles.

I had a quiet word with a member of the management and asked him if that meant what I thought it meant. He nodded so I knew my chances of going were slim. It was a long week.

I can't complain too much about missing the 2007 World Cup. But the fact that I didn't go, the fact that four years later I battled through a shoulder injury in double quick time in 2011, only made that fall-out from the ankle ligament injury so much worse.

I felt my weight problems were well under control by 2011 and was certain I could have really contributed to that World Cup campaign. Instead, I spent the autumn slogging my guts out to come back from yet another injury.

With that hard work behind me, I was desperate to try to break back into the Wales squad for the 2012 Six Nations tournament. I needed everything I could grasp to convince Warren Gatland I was worthy of bringing back into the fold.

What I did not need was to be criticised by my own Ospreys coach, which was exactly what happened.

Scott Johnson – Jonno – was always a reporter's dream – a one-man walking headline. He used to open his mouth and the hacks would their fill their boots. But he normally had a clever way of winding up the opposition, rather than his own players.

I was left out of the initial Wales squad named for the championship. Smiler (Matthew Rees), Benny (Huw Bennett) and Ken Owens were the hookers named, but I was still desperate to force my way back in. So it didn't exactly help my cause when Jonno sounded off at an Ospreys press conference that I still had a weight issue. He dressed it up in some flowery phrases but the nub of it was that I was too fat to get picked for Wales.

I had worked my backside off to get fit from the ankle injury. I had put up with shoulder problems flaring up again. I had had cortisone injections three times that season so that I could carry on playing in big games for the Ospreys ... Johnson's Ospreys.

To hear the bloke come out with something like that was a hard pill to swallow. That's how he had decided to repay me.

I texted him and asked what the hell he was playing at. He must have sensed my anger because he told me to come and see him straight away.

What had really angered me was his lack of appreciation for me slogging my guts out for his team. It didn't seem to have occurred to him. Neither did he seem to realise that mud sticks. The Welsh public have a habit of remembering stuff like this. Any negative judgements are clung on to for ever and a day. I knew that I would be getting stick for a long time to come – and I was right – because I'd seen it happen before.

I also knew that once you get a reputation in rugby it's very hard to shift it and even the most sensible people can be swayed.

None of this had entered Jonno's head. He claimed he had been misquoted, but that was rubbish. I didn't hold back in the meeting, but the man refused to back down.

He always had this way of trapping you in riddles and he did it again. It was like wrestling an octopus. You think you've got him but he's always got a free arm to try another move. He's loose with his tongue, but very good at shifting an argument around so that suddenly it feels as though it's you who's in the wrong. But he's likeable with it. He makes it hard to hate him.

But that day he definitely knew he had touched a nerve. I was bouncing.

Coaches often don't seem to recognise the damage their remarks can cause. They should stick to firing off at the opposition. That doesn't bother players in the slightest. Any other coach, player, fan – whoever – can spout insults about me and I couldn't care less. But when it's your own coach, the guy you have a close working relationship with, it hurts.

Wales went on to win their first two games of the 2012 Six Nations championship –

matches I had to watch, feeling like an outsider.

I was then drafted in to sit on the bench for the match against England at Twickenham. Wales won again 19–12 thanks to a fantastic individual try by Scott Williams, but I didn't get on and when that happens you never feel fully part of it.

It's a strange feeling. You are part of the squad, part of the group that has trained and prepared, and if you get on the field you feel part of the victory. But when you just watch the whole match from the bench you feel detached. You're there – but you're not really there. You celebrate, but it's not the same feeling as the others enjoy.

Then Matthew Rees came back in for the Italy and France matches – with Ken Owens back on the bench – and I went back out of the squad.

Nobody thinks much about players who are left out when Wales are winning. Why should they? It's only natural to focus on the guys who are doing the business out on the field.

But time doesn't stop for those on the outside looking in. You have to keep going – make the best of things. But it's hard. I'm one of those players who wants to play every week. Even if I'm rested for a game, some part of me feels like I've been dropped.

So, when Wales won that 2012 Grand Slam I wasn't in the squad that clinched it by beating France 16–9. Three weeks before I had sat on the bench at Twickenham, but when Wales lifted the trophy that night in the Millennium Stadium, and the players sprayed champagne, I watched it all in a Wetherspoons pub in Port Talbot.

I could have gone to the stadium and watched from the stands, but I'm one of those players who finds it hard to be around the game if I'm not actually required to play. I feel like a spare part. I didn't want to be suited and booted and paraded around when I'd done nothing to deserve it or feel part of it. So I watched it in a pub with my mates.

It's just as hard for the replacements who don't get on the field, and sometimes even for those who do get on, but only for a few minutes at the end. If you play less than twenty-five minutes, the coaching staff make you run fitness drills in the empty stadium after everyone else has gone home. Talk about soul-destroying and demoralising.

There are always some lingering drunks around who stand and stare and shout abuse. Believe me, it's a tough gig.

My only consolation was that the Ospreys won the Pro12 title in that 2012 season – our second championship in three years and fourth win in eight years. I had been a big part of that campaign and felt justifiably proud of what we had achieved.

It was a good season for us and we won the final in style by beating Leinster in Dublin – denying them a domestic and European double. Predictably, Shane Williams bowed out at the very top by scoring the vital late try and Dan Biggar kicked the winning points.

We celebrated well that night, but within a week I was back in the Wales squad for the summer tour to Australia. I didn't know it at the time, but it would prove to be one of the worst times I've gone through as a rugby player – maybe even worse than the injury that put me out of the 2011 World Cup.

I wasn't involved in the first Test, which the Wallabies won 27–19. Matthew started at hooker with Ken on the bench. It sounds close, but it wasn't. We looked tired.

I played against the Brumbies in the

midweek game, which went well, and then got back on the bench for the second Test in Melbourne. Things were looking up.

The game was close all the way through and when I finally got on, replacing Matthew, Leigh Halfpenny had just kicked a penalty to put us 23–22 ahead with fifteen minutes to go. After so many near misses in the previous seasons, Wales were about to finally get another southern hemisphere scalp. We just had to hold out to beat the Aussies.

The score stayed that way until the final minute of the game. There was a kick down midfield and then a ruck just outside their 22. Then the ref had me for diving over and a penalty was given.

They kicked to touch and drove a maul down the field. It collapsed and I was penalised for bringing it down. I felt it was harsh, brutal. But there was nothing I could do.

I knew what was coming. But it was still horrible to watch. I'll never forget the look on the boys' faces as the ref made that call and we trudged back towards our posts.

Australia's replacement Mike Harris kicked the penalty, the ref blew for the end of the match, and Australia had won 25–23. I felt sick.

I don't remember walking to the dressing room, but I do remember that no one spoke to me when we got inside. Maybe Jug-head (Ryan Jones) might have mumbled some words of comfort, but that was it. The rest were silent. It was awful.

It wasn't my best night. I had conceded the penalty that allowed Australia to deny us our victory. But it was about to get worse. At the next team meeting, Rob Howley – who was head coach on that tour while Warren Gatland prepared for the Lions – announced that the teams for the third and final Test would be the same. Then he named the replacements – one by one. I was the only change. I'd been dropped from the bench. It could not have been more painfully spelt out – the defeat was down to me.

That was a blow I didn't need. I'd already had a guts-full of hate on Twitter – complete strangers hurling abuse at me, telling me I should never play for Wales again. You take the rough with the smooth as a professional, but that kind of stuff is disheartening.

I had a bad night. I thought of everything that had gone wrong for me in that year: the injury on the eve of the World Cup; the criticism from Scott Johnson, having to watch the Grand Slam in a pub. And now this – blamed and shamed for handing victory to Australia.

I was on the other side of the world and felt it – a long way from Lou and the girls. That's it, I thought. I'm not going to play international rugby again. I wasn't giving up. I just thought I was accepting the inevitable, that I would never be picked again. Every time I had a chance something always went horribly wrong.

Wales also lost the third Test – cruelly close again, 20–19 – to end the series. At least I wasn't involved in that so no one could say it was my fault. I helped Ian Evans celebrate his recent honeymoon and tried to forget my feeling that I'd never play for Wales again.

When I got back home I began training again and found myself working hard. I didn't quite know why. But then I realised I wasn't finished with international rugby after all.

I wanted to prove to people that I was better than that ... better than that year ... better than 2012 and its injuries and upset. I could get past all that, I thought. So, I started to train hard, with extra sessions on my own in the gym in the evening.

I dropped some weight – about two or three

kilos – and began the 2012–13 season early for the Ospreys and with a sense of purpose. The new state of mind lasted through the summer and into the autumn. I was also feeling the benefit of that weight loss. It wasn't huge but I felt faster and more able to maintain energy levels.

Huw Bennett left that summer to play in France, and the Ospreys had injury issues with other hookers. So I was playing early in the season and staying on for the full eighty minutes. It did me good.

I was playing well and got into the Wales squad for the 2012 autumn internationals, which began with a training camp in Poland. I hadn't gone there the first time – just before the 2011 World Cup – so this was a first visit for me. I don't recommend it.

I could cope with the cryogenic ice chambers, but it was the atmosphere and the routine at that camp in Spala that really left me cold. It felt more like a prisoner of war camp than a training facility.

I can remember being woken at 5 a.m. on a freezing morning to go to a swimming session. I'd had an awful night's sleep, it was bitterly cold, and I swim like a brick. Yet here I was in a swimming cap, trying to do lengths while genuine Polish swimmers stood around staring at me. It wasn't fun at all – and unnecessary.

I was on the bench for the first game of the autumn – against Argentina – and although we lost 26–12, at least I didn't give any penalties away.

I was then picked to start against Samoa. At the first line-out I ran around the corner and hit a bus. At least that's what it felt like. This Samoan guy hit me so hard on my left-hand side that I sprung a joint in my shoulder. The pain was so intense it went through my left shoulder, across, and down the right side of my body. It felt as though I had been electrocuted.

It was a brutal match and we suffered a load of injuries. I managed to keep going for twenty minutes, but I couldn't pick my arm up. I remember trucking the ball up and thinking, there's something wrong here. My arm isn't working.

Another Wales game ended in injury and we ended up losing 26–19. I was then ruled out of the games against New Zealand and Australia, which also ended in defeat. On reflection, maybe they weren't bad matches to miss, although I certainly didn't feel like that at the time.

I came back three weeks ahead of schedule to play for for the Ospreys in the Heineken Cup and we beat Toulouse at home in an amazing game. Thankfully, my form returned straight away and I felt well placed for the 2013 Six Nations, until I suffered another shoulder injury playing against Leicester.

It felt like bad luck had struck again as I missed the opening game of the tournament against Ireland. Carcass (Mark Davies) had looked at the injury and thought I wasn't going to make the Ireland game, so he downed plenty of wine at dinner before plucking up the courage to tell me. We must have had a deep, meaningful conversation for about an hour and a half.

I really thought this international rugby business was just not meant for me. I was never going to make it. I had a long conversation with Lou where I doubted whether this was all worth it, the pain, the heartache, the frustration.

Strangely, though, I felt positive again the next morning. I felt I could get fit for the match against France. I didn't know why the feeling came that morning, and I couldn't say why now, either, but I woke up feeling OK about life. It was a turning point that came out of nowhere, but just how big a transformation I had absolutely no idea.

Chapter Six

ON TOP WITH WALES – AND THE LIONS!

Wales lost their opening match of the 2013 Six Nations 30–22 at home to Ireland. The team didn't play well but of greater significance for the critics was the fact that it was the eighth defeat on the trot and so Rob Howley came in for plenty of stick.

Perhaps the sequence was significant for me, too, because when the team to play France was announced, I was named as hooker. I'd recovered from my shoulder problem, just as Carcass had promised, and came straight into the starting line-up.

I was twenty-nine. This was my twentieth Wales cap, over a six-year period, and yet this was my first start in a Six Nations international. It felt like a new beginning.

It also felt like a reward for all the hard work I had put in since coming back from Australia. I had jumped a hurdle.

I had been on the bench out in Paris before, so I knew it would be a special experience. I wasn't wrong. It's a great stadium, the Stade de France, and the crowd make a fantastic atmosphere.

The build-up had been intense because so many people seemed to be on Howler's (Rob Howley's) back. The pressure was building and you could sense that some people back home were sharpening the knives.

No one gave us a chance against what was considered a decent French side, who would be looking for revenge after shockingly losing to Italy in Rome.

The pace of the game was so much quicker than I'd been used to that season, but I felt I did OK. I came off after fifty-five minutes, pretty much to plan, when we were level at 6–6 but just starting to feel more comfortable as the game wore on.

The match seemed to be drifting towards a draw when George North suddenly scored a try out of nothing. Leigh Halfpenny kicked the conversion, then added a penalty, and before long we had won 16–6.

It's a game remembered for George's father, David, who ran on the pitch to hug his son seconds after he'd scored. None of us knew it was his dad. I assumed it was just some random lunatic, and when we found out the truth it was hilarious. We toasted his old man with a few beers in the bar later, but it was not a big night. There was still a lot of work to be done in that championship.

There was no new secret formula to that victory. We just did what we had done in the previous games and finally it fell for us, thanks to the luck of a bounce.

But the change within the squad was huge. There was a surge of confidence and we all couldn't wait for the next game, which was Italy.

It hammered it down that day in Rome. My first throw was meant to be a big 25-yarder into the hands of Jamie Roberts. But we messed it up in the rain and for a moment I thought I might be about to have one of those days.

Nothing to worry about, though. We started to dominate all the set pieces and Italy just didn't know what to do. We ended up comfy winners, 26–9.

I felt happy enough as my performance had been a step up from the French match. I was feeling at ease as a starting international hooker. Ok, I'd learned that I couldn't expect to do quite as much around the field as I did for the

Ospreys. But that was more down to the sheer speed of Test rugby than anything else. Robin McBryde, our forwards coach, seemed pleased enough with my contribution. He had a few brief "work-ons" and that was that. On to the next one, which was Scotland, again away from home. I was picked to start again – my third consecutive appearance in the side that took the field, although the nerves and the butterflies beforehand didn't feel any less. I certainly wasn't thinking about Lions tours or anything of that sort before we went to Murrayfield. It was all about the next game ... the next scrum ... the next line-out.

But the media weren't taking one game at a time. That's not their style. The newspapers were all full of how a convincing victory over Scotland would set up a winner-takes-all clash with England for the title. It seemed far-fetched to me, simply because their points difference was far greater than ours and they had Italy to play the day after we met the Scots.

Scotland gave us a tough afternoon. It was made more difficult, I think, because Scott Johnson was now coaching them and he knew so much about all our Ospreys players – me included. At least he didn't try to get inside my head in the build-up. I was half-expecting a few hand grenades, but Jonno was quiet. Perhaps he had enough on his plate with a new squad of players.

We beat Scotland 28–18 and I managed to score my first international try that day. Someone made a break, we won four or five more phases, and I finally got my hands on the ball to power over. It wasn't a great distance to the line, but I still needed a big push from behind by Alun Wyn Jones to get me over.

It was an amazing feeling. To score a try for Wales is a high that's hard to describe … like walking on air. It also was a big match for me because I felt so much more at home on the field. I did more work around the pitch, carried the ball more often, and, significantly, I stayed on for a bit longer, too. It felt good.

We expected England to put 40 points on Italy the next day, but they very nearly lost. I couldn't believe what I was watching. It had everyone looking at the points totals and adding things up. It was simple, really. A week later we would need to beat England by eight points to retain the Six Nations championship title.

In the week leading into that England game, the approach outlined was to win the game first and only worry about points margins after we felt the victory was secure. It was gaining the victory that was the priority.

I loved the week, the build-up, the full-on feeling of Wales against England. It's what you dream about as a kid. I found I could switch off when I needed to – watch a film – but then switch back on when I wanted to focus on what I had to do, my roles in the team.

I like to stay in bed late on match day, have breakfast as late as possible, then try to relax and stay calm. We had a forwards meeting – the calm before the storm – and then it started to build. Some of the boys like to get so pumped up that you can't even talk to them, but I like to keep my mind occupied on other things.

Going from the Vale of Glamorgan Hotel to the centre of Cardiff on the team bus – especially on Wales–England match day – is awesome. The fans are going mad, screaming and shouting at you from windows, all willing you on to beat England. It's something to savour, something you want to bottle and take with you into the battle.

The crowd that day, under the closed roof, was incredible. You soak it all up beforehand, breathe it all in like vapour, and then try to stay just on top of your emotions. Then, when the game starts you blank it all out. It's as if they're not there.

The match itself was brutal – so fast, intense and exhausting. I remember looking up at the clock, thinking we were midway through the first half, but only twelve minutes had gone. I wondered how I was going to last.

Bits of the match stay in my mind ... fragments, really. Like rushing out of the defensive line to put a big hit on the England prop Joe Marler. I heard the crowd react as I connected.

But the speed of the match was astonishing. It went by in a blur. We unleashed a battery on them and just kept pummelling. We were giving them a hard time in the scrums and they weren't happy. Their forwards were moaning at Steve Walsh, the referee, but he wasn't interested in their complaints.

They were getting beaten at every scrum. At every hit, they would go down because I don't think they could deal with the power coming through. It's a great feeling. You know you have the edge, you know the ref knows it, and you know that you're likely to win a penalty because they can't handle the pressure.

England's complaints told me they were getting flustered. At one point the scrum collapsed, Dan Cole landed on top of me, and he tried to choke me. We laughed about it later on the Lions tour.

I went off midway through the second half and for once I was happy to go. I was empty. I had nothing left. I knew I'd be replaced at about that stage, so I made sure I'd given everything.

I actually went and sat on my own in the dressing room for five minutes to recover. By the time I came back out, we were 27–3 up and coasting. Justin Tipuric – who was something else that day – created a second try for Alex Cuthbert and then Dan Biggar took it to 30–3 with a late penalty.

To beat England by that much, and win the championship, felt unbelievable. It was the biggest winning margin ever by a Welsh side against the English. But the moment that really sticks in my mind was when they turned out all the lights in the stadium just before we lifted the trophy. I could feel the presence of 75,000 people, as if they were sitting on my chest. It made me tremble. Then the lights came on, the fireworks exploded, and everyone went nuts as Ryan Jones, in a suit and with one arm in a sling, helped lift up the Six Nations trophy with Gethin Jenkins.

There's almost no time to savour things. You parade the trophy, go in for photos, get changed into your dinner suits, and head for the official function.

The night itself was an anticlimax, if I'm honest. You'd imagine it's the party to beat all parties, but most of us older boys, and the couples, went back to the hotel. I was too exhausted to move. Only the younger boys went out on the town.

I was too tired to drink much, but when I finally went to bed I was too excited to sleep. I felt as if I had really contributed to that Six Nations title – as if I'd really been part of it. I'd never felt like that before, not with Wales. I'd finally crossed a busy road, without getting knocked down.

A few people suggested I was now in the running to make the Lions squad for the tour to Australia, but I didn't believe it myself. There were plenty of other good hookers around.

The rest of my season went OK with the Ospreys until the injury jinx struck again when I hurt my knee playing against Glasgow. I almost laughed as I came off the pitch – laughed like a madman.

It's happened again, I thought. If I was in any kind of running for a Lions tour spot, then I've just had it flushed down the drain. I hate going off injured – unless I can hardly walk, I won't – and this was the case then.

But it was a week before the Lions squad was to be announced, and no one knew how serious my knee injury might be. I didn't want a scan. I just wanted to see how it might respond to a couple of injections.

The day of the Lions announcement I watched it like everyone else on Sky Sports. It's brilliant for viewers, but for players it's a nightmare. You sit there listening to Andy Irvine, the Lions team manager, read out a list of names. He was slow and methodical. It was torture. I was lying on my bed, with my bad knee throbbing.

Then he said it ... Richard Hibbard. The buzz of hearing my name almost lifted me up to the ceiling. My phone went into meltdown, and I started to dream about what might lie ahead. Then, very quickly afterwards, I got a sobering feeling as I thought about my injured knee.

I spent the next few days pretending my knee was fine. I went to a press conference and took my knee brace off in the car to make out there was nothing wrong with me. I tried hard not to walk with too much of a limp.

The Lions soon met up in London and it felt like the first day at a new school. You mix with people you don't know, about to live in each others' pockets. I looked around and took in how many great players were there. It was intimidating.

We were fitted out with all our clothes and gear and only then, when they give you your bags with your name emblazoned on it, do you realise it's true – you're going on a Lions tour.

But I still had to get through the medical, otherwise I'd be going nowhere. There was an insurance agent in the room, as well as two doctors, and when they bent my knee and saw how lax the joint was, all three of them looked at each other.

They asked to look at my other knee and when they discovered that one was just as loose, they became less tense. Perhaps they thought I was double-jointed! I laughed nervously and somehow got the all-clear.

My memory of that whole period is a little sketchy. I was still terrified about that first Lions camp training session and whether my knee would stand the rigours of full contact. I knew that if it collapsed under me there would be no Lions tour and I'd be back staring blankly into darkness for the umpteenth time.

It didn't, though. It was fine. I could relax and start getting to know my new squad-mates. We had a good two weeks before a final session at Twickenham – which was pretty low quality and Gats (Warren Gatland) let us know about it – before we prepared to fly out to Hong Kong for the opening leg of the tour.

I can normally cope with a bit of heat and humidity, but Hong Kong that week was unlike anything I'd ever experienced. One of the other boys summed it up when he described an afternoon training session as like running with a hairdryer pointing towards your face.

On one of the early nights there, we all went out for a few beers in order for everyone from the four countries to get to know each other a little better. It was a good idea for the squad, but a bad idea for me personally. The next morning at training I felt I was having an out-of-body experience.

It was 35 degrees and 90 per cent humidity, and I was dehydrated. Gats looked at the state I was in and told me to sit out for a few minutes. I felt really awful.

We tried everything that week – ice vests, mists, cold patches on our wrists – anything to try and cool our body temperatures. But it was hard graft – and so was the first game.

We beat the Barbarians 59–8 and I was very happy and relieved I'd begun as the starting hooker. Not as relieved as I was to get out of the oven and fly down to Australia, though.

In all, I played in nine out of the ten matches on the tour – only Dan Cole matched that figure – and it was the rugby highlight of my career. But it was tough, too. You are on a constant treadmill of travel ... train ... play ... travel ... train ... play. You are never settled, never fully relaxed. If you're not packing, you're unpacking. Training was mostly short and sharp, simply because there was never time for long sessions.

I never had much time off, because I was playing so often. But that was fine. I wouldn't change that. I'm always happier playing than not playing – always have been. I saw a bit of Australia, and the insides of a few cinemas, but only in hours snatched here and there.

Tom Youngs started at hooker for the game against Queensland Reds and I was on the bench. The same thing happened against the Waratahs.

They were the two big ones – the ones you wanted to play in if you had hopes of making the Test team. I was disappointed because I knew what the selections meant, but I wasn't downhearted.

On the Wednesday before the first Test against the Wallabies, Gats named his team at the Hilton Hotel in Brisbane. I sat down in the team room and put my hood up over my head. Then I heard it – Youngs at hooker, Hibbard on the bench. It was a crushing blow, but it could have been worse, I suppose. I could have missed out altogether. The boys who are outside the squad, they're the ones with the toughest job for the rest of the week – holding tackle bags and trying not to let their seething resentment spread into the squad itself. At least relations between myself, Tom and Rory Best were good and they stayed that way for the rest of the tour. I thought they were both great guys, despite the rivalry for the same position.

We won the first Test 23–21, but we could so easily have lost it. Mako Vunipola gave away a penalty very late on and I had a terrible flashback to a year ago, when I'd done the same against the Wallabies. Not again, I thought. But Kurtley Beale slipped over as he kicked the penalty and we hung on for the win.

We were happy to have won and I was delighted to have got on and played my part in the victory. But it wasn't really us. It wasn't the same side that had physically battered teams in the warm-up games. There was a brilliant individual battle between George North and the Wallaby wing Israel Folau, but we had eased up and they'd very nearly sneaked past us.

After the game the Lions forwards coach, Graham Rowntree, got all the forward replacements together and tore into us. Our impact off the bench hadn't been good enough, he said. Now I was worried I might not even make the bench for the second Test in Melbourne, but I wasn't alone in having those fears.

Although we had won, it felt a bit like defeat because we knew how easily that could have been the actual outcome. Certain players were now piping up here and there, having their say, as though a good rousing speech might get them into the Test team. I've always been a bit suspicious of those types. Too often, I've seen them talk like Tarzan and then play like Jane.

I stayed on the bench for the Melbourne Test, which the Aussies won 16–15 to square the series. For a team on the back foot, the Wallabies responded well. All credit to them. Their scrum was improved and they seemed to get the rub of the green with some interpretations by the referee.

I came on to play the last twenty-four minutes and felt I'd done OK, but collectively we were guilty of being too negative – waiting for the whistle to come as we defended our lead, until all of a sudden the lead was gone and the game was over.

But Gats was calm afterwards and, looking back, I think that was a shrewd reaction. He paid credit to the Wallabies, but told us that they had reached their peak. They had thrown everything at us and had won by only a point to make it 1–1. Now, he said, came the decider and we would raise it up a level to where they couldn't go. We'd destroy them, he insisted.

On selection day before the third Test, Wig (Graham Rowntree) pulled me to one side and told me I was starting. I was shocked. I hadn't guessed that they would change things.

But then the rest of the team was made known, and I could see what the plan was. It was a more physical team. We were going out to batter them into submission.

On the Thursday before the Sydney Test, up

at our getaway spot at Noosa, I had a shocker of a training session. The line-outs went poorly, boys were dropping balls and everyone was getting tetchy. I messed up a move, then didn't hear when Johnny Sexton changed the call for the next move. That one was a shambles and Johnny went nuts.

I took it for a while – let him sound off at me – and then needed all my willpower to hold back because I wanted to kill him. For a few seconds my anger took over and if he had been nearer who knows what would have happened? It blew over pretty quickly but the last thing I needed was my No.10 bawling at me.

Johnny went on to play a stormer on the Saturday, and he had a great tour, but I think we had both poured all our anxieties and nerves into that flash-point and it ignited. Thankfully, a wise word from Rob Howley settled me down.

Before that deciding final Test, I was more nervous than I had ever been in my life. It all boiled down to this and I was just so desperate not to let anyone down.

The build-up was tense, so tense. Few words were spoken. Everyone knew what was at stake. But there was something about the whole day that felt perfect – the weather, the journey to the ANZ Stadium, the atmosphere inside the ground.

It started perfectly, right from the moment Will Genia dropped the ball in the first few seconds and we piled into the ruck. We smashed into them and soon scored the opening try through Alex Corbisiero.

Then came the moment that most people recall about my Lions tour – my tackle on George Smith. I could see him run through on the angle, Alun Wyn half scragged him, and then I just smashed into him. In truth, I bounced back off him and I was fuming I'd been the one to get knocked back.

I jumped straight back up and didn't feel any pain, even though our heads had collided at full force. But I looked down and Smith was on the floor. He wasn't getting up, either, and I felt happy with that. I had leapt back up, because he'd bounced me, but it was soon obvious he'd come off a lot worse.

When he eventually went off, with two physios holding him up, he did the old snake dance because he simply couldn't walk straight. Sexton ran over and patted me on the back and I knew it was a significant moment.

A few minutes later, we had a scrum in their

half. We pushed hard and then everything went black and I was lying on the ground. I'd passed out. I didn't know where I was or what day it was. The Lions doctor, James Robson, suddenly came into vision in front of me and thankfully I remembered where I was.

I don't think it was down to the Smith tackle, but you never know. I've fainted before after scrums because at hooker you can sometimes have your oxygen supply cut off for a time as your arms are spread wide out.

Fair play to Smith, though. A few minutes later he was running back on. He's a great player and a very hard man because it would have been easy for him to fail the mandatory pitch-side concussion test if he had wanted to. The question, more, is how did he manage to pass it?

The fact that he was allowed to return would later be a big talking point and the debate over the effects of concussion has rumbled on. Later I'd feel glad he was OK but at the time I was just pleased he wasn't that effective when he came back on. I watched him play a match a couple of weeks later and he won it on his own. He's a phenomenal player.

After blacking out, I spent the rest of the match in a bit of a haze. I chucked myself about for another forty minutes or so, and then finally came off after about fifty minutes. I was shattered. I couldn't lift my arms. My shoulders were wrecked and my neck ached.

I had some oxygen in the dressing room because I was feeling dizzy and then came back out after about sixty minutes, by which time we were winning comfortably. Sexton, George North and Jamie Roberts scored tries and the game was over. There was no catching us.

I went to applaud one of them with a clap above my head, but felt the pain shoot down my shoulders and thought better of it.

My body was in bits. It's something that worries me when I allow myself the time to think about it. By the time I'm fifty my body will be in pieces, I know that. I have trouble sleeping most nights and my hands often feel numb.

But you do it for nights like that one in Sydney. Nights you'll never forget. Nights when the scoreboard reads Australia 16, British and Irish Lions 41.

After the game, Daniel Craig came into the dressing room and we all swigged from champagne bottles, while having our pictures taken with James Bond. He gave me a big hug and congratulated me. I think I spent the next five minutes following him around like a puppy, while all the other boys were jumping up and down. He was great – he seemed genuinely thrilled to be amongst us and we even sang some Bond theme tunes.

As the Lions we had spent ten weeks fighting our way around Australia, fighting each other for places in the team, and suddenly we were in the moment we had wanted together – screaming and sharing what we all knew would be a special day in our lives.

I'm thankful that I later got to spend some time with Lou. It also felt special to be with the person who matters most.

On Sunday, I met up with the boys who were over from Taibach rugby club and then on Monday a few of the Lions went out for one last dinner on the eve of our flight home. We played credit card roulette to pay the bill and guess who lost? My winning streak was over.

But it had been a momentous year for me. I was a Six Nations title-winner with Wales and had been part of a Lions team which had won a series for the first time in sixteen years. I had conquered my fears. I had realised my dreams. I'd learnt a lot about myself, even though some things remained unresolved. Now it was time to go home and spend time with Louise and the girls, Tiella and Summer, get some well-earned rest, and face whatever new challenges and adventures were on the horizon.

Quick Reads 📖

Books in the Quick Reads series

101 Ways to get your Child to Read	Patience Thomson
A Day to Remember	Fiona Phillips
Aim High	Tanni Grey-Thompson
Alive and Kicking	Andy Legg
All These Lonely People	Gervase Phinn
Amy's Diary	Maureen Lee
Be Your Own Boss	Alison Stokes
Beyond the Bounty	Tony Parsons
Black-Eyed Devils	Catrin Collier
Bloody Valentine	James Patterson
Bring it Back Home	Niall Griffiths
Buster Fleabags	Rolf Harris
The Corpse's Tale	Katherine John
Chickenfeed	Minette Walters
The Cleverness of Ladies	Alexander McCall Smith
Clouded Vision	Linwood Barclay
A Cool Head	Ian Rankin
Danny Wallace and the Centre of the Universe	Danny Wallace
The Dare	John Boyne
Doctor Who: Code of the Krillitanes	Justin Richards
Doctor Who: Made of Steel	Terrance Dicks
Doctor Who: Magic of the Angels	Jacqueline Rayner
Doctor Who: Revenge of the Judoon	Terrance Dicks
Do Not Go Gentle	Phil Carradice
Dragons' Den: Your Road to Success	
A Dream Come True	Maureen Lee
Earnie – My Life at Cardiff City	Robert Earnshaw
Finding Myself Lost	Richard J Oliver
Finger Food	Helen Lederer
The Flying Pineapple	Jamie Baulch
Follow Me	Sheila O'Flanagan
Full House	Maeve Binchy
Get the Life You Really Want	James Caan
Girl on the Platform	Josephine Cox
Going for Gold	
Grand Slam Man	Dan Lydiate